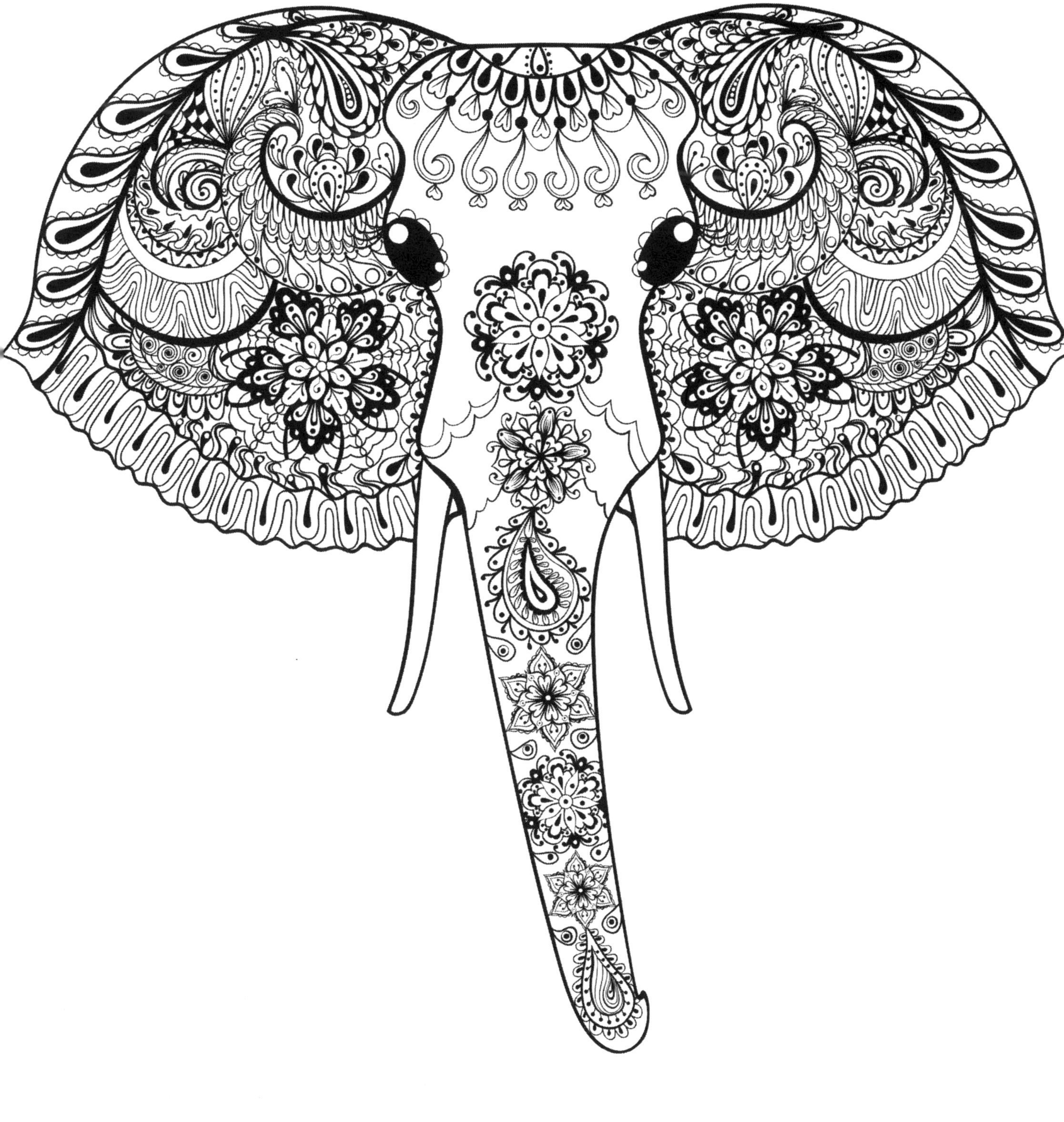

# Getting Started Coloring!

Bring out your imagination, arouse your senses and creativity, and as you become engaged in the pleasurable, soothing activity of Coloring, it calms you and instantaneously starts reducing your stress level.

This book is a wonderful addition to your coloring library; a perfect gift school aged children, college students, or adults who enjoy coloring, and a much easier way to reduce stress than going to the gym.

In this Elegant Elephant Coloring Book For Adults We bring to you great & Elephant Drawing that you can start Coloring Now. These elegant Animals are so richly hand-drawn, after you are finished, you'll have lovely works of art that are worthy of hanging on the wall. You won't need to have the skills of an artist to personalize these intricate drawings.

The complexity and details vary with the pictures, some you will need sharpened colored pencils or Gel pens for and others crayons or wide markers would work. Place a piece of scrap paper under the page you are coloring in case your pens or markers bleed through the page.

*Happy Coloring... :)*

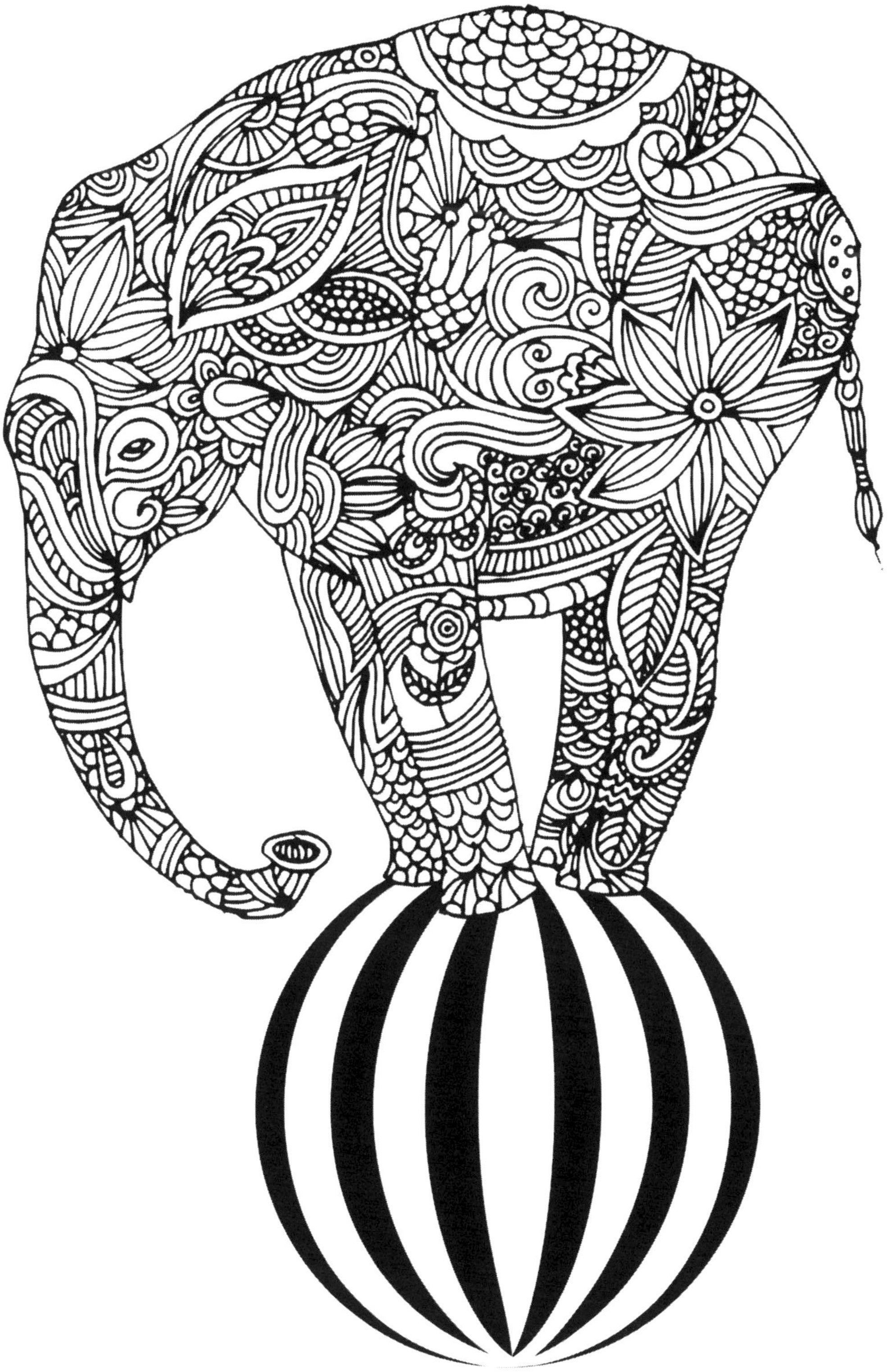

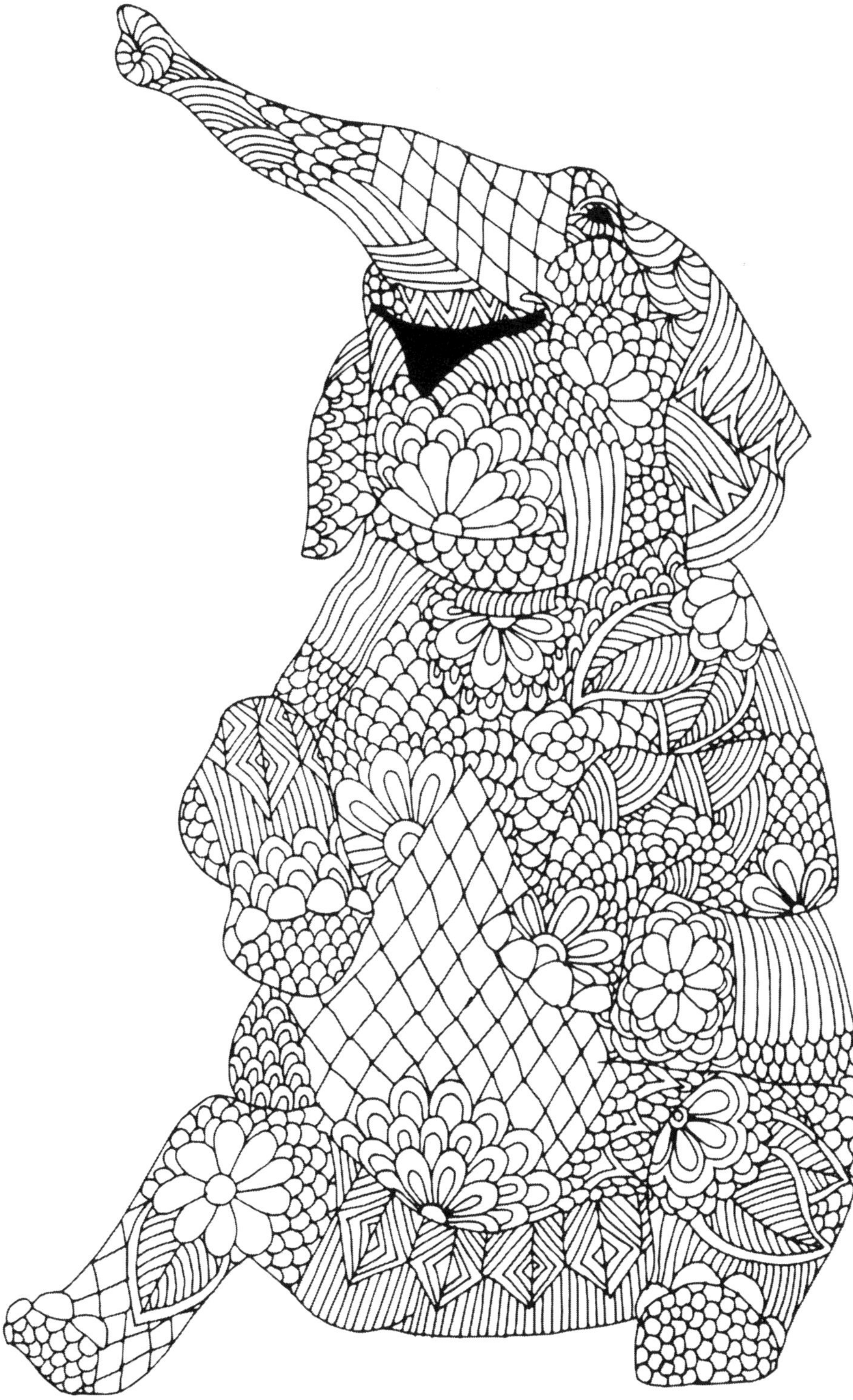

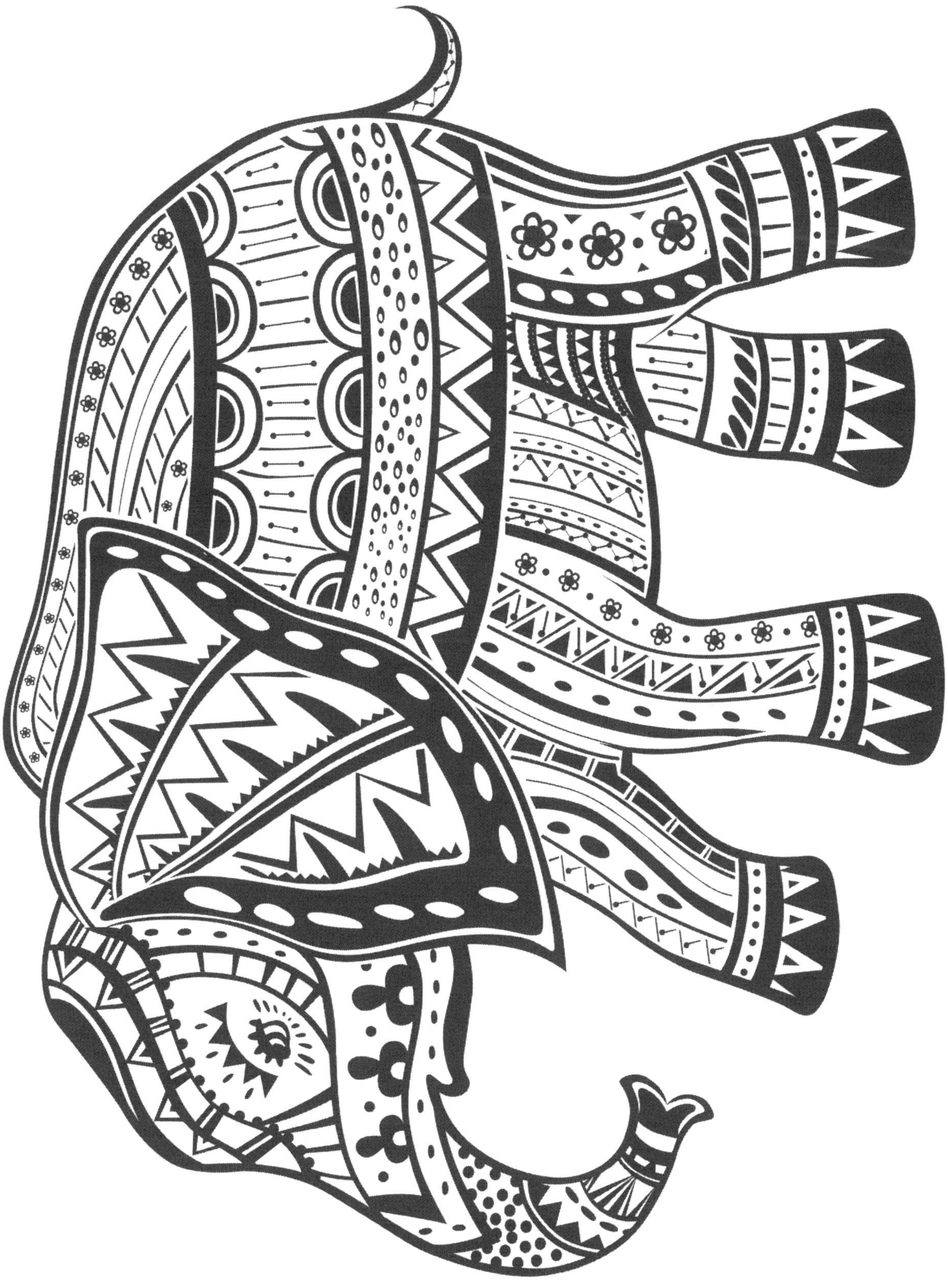

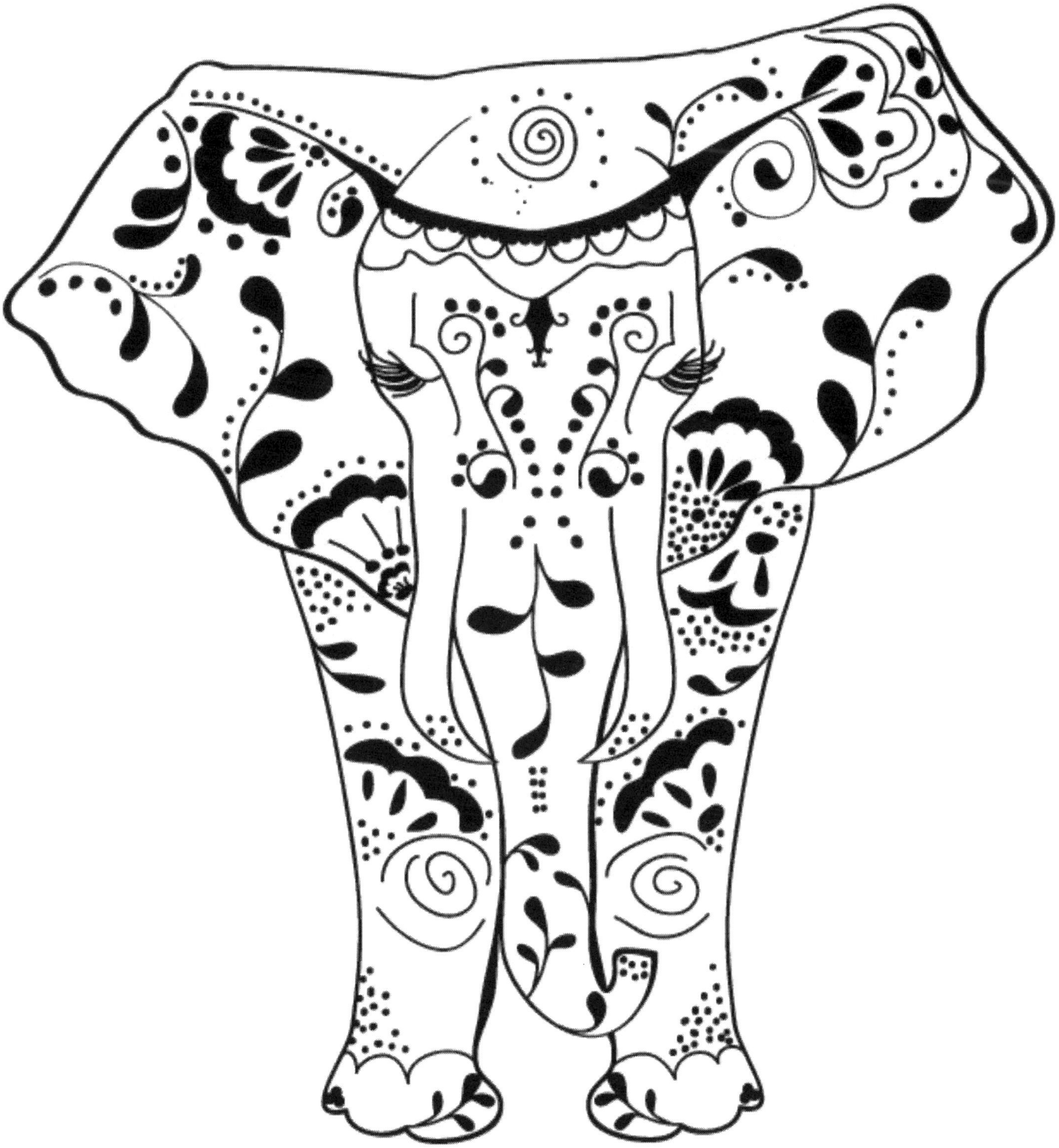

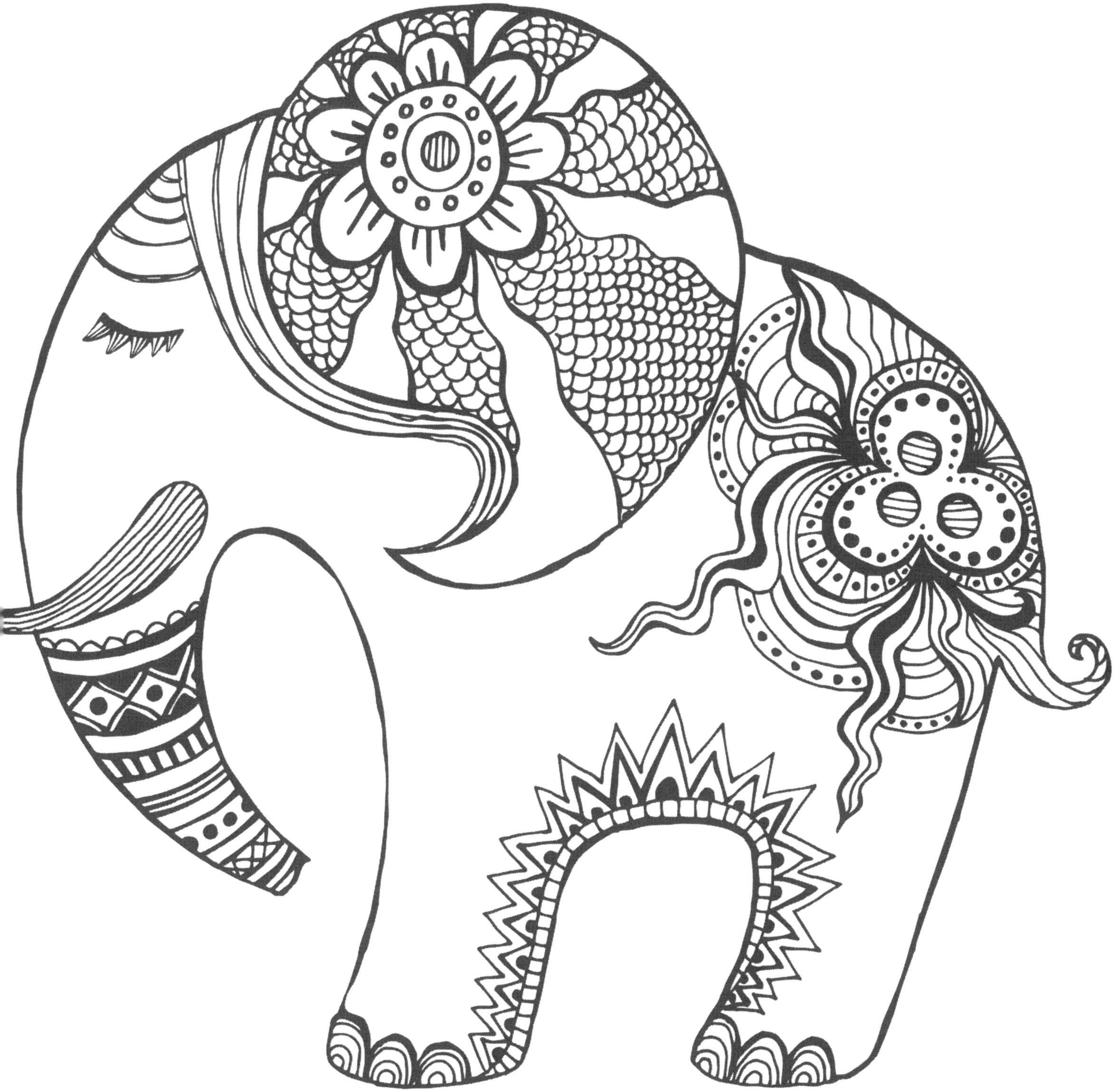

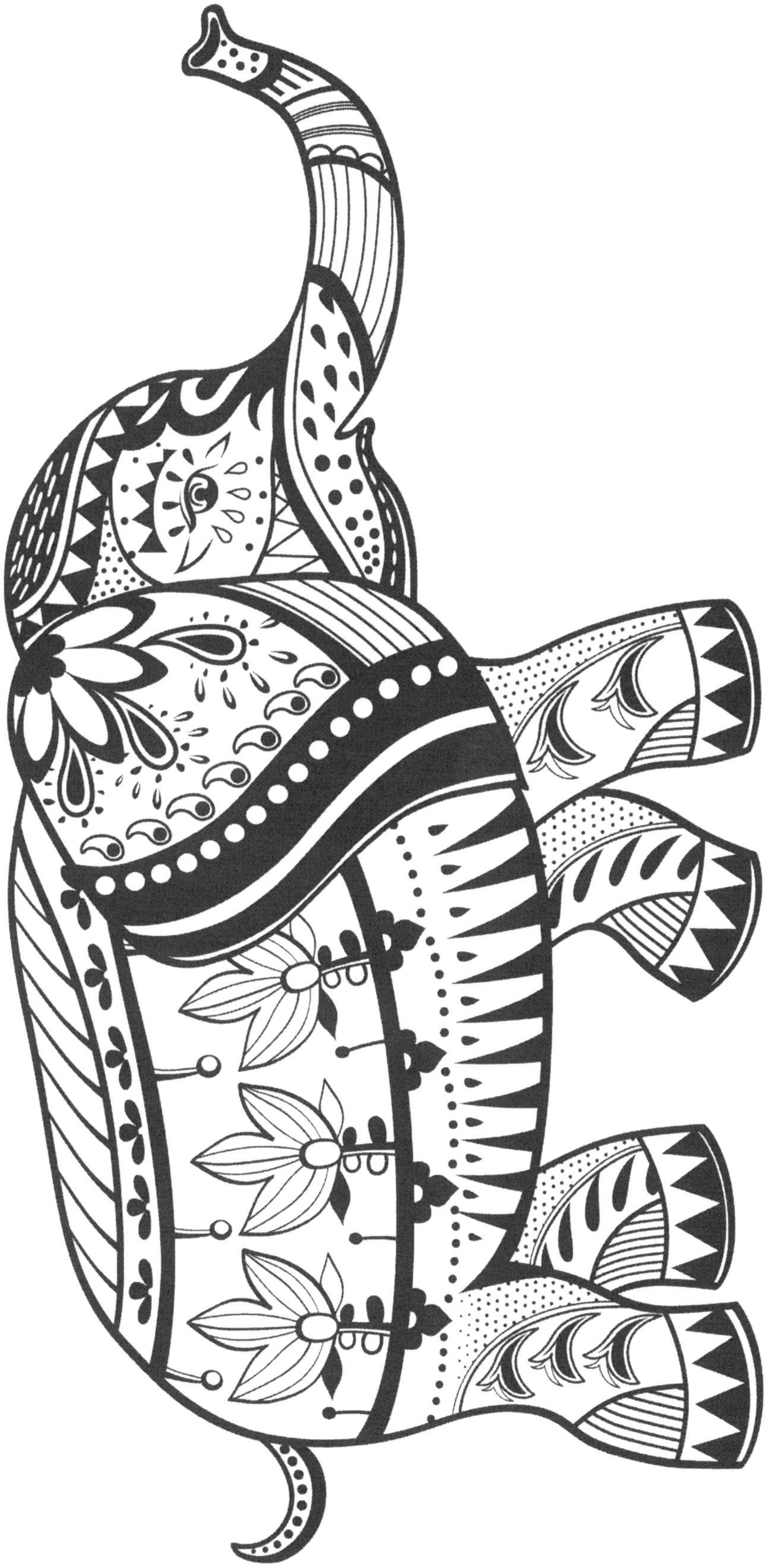

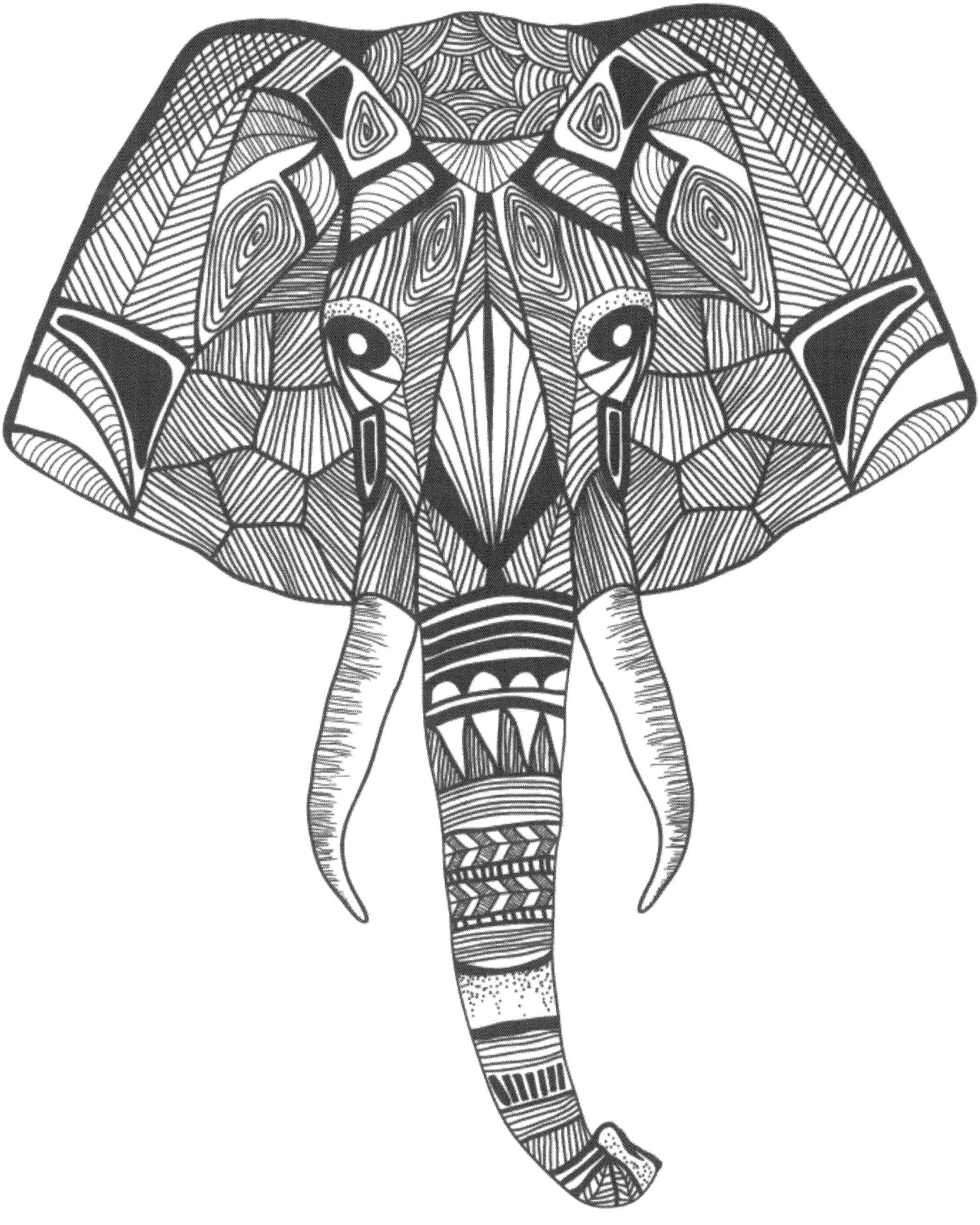

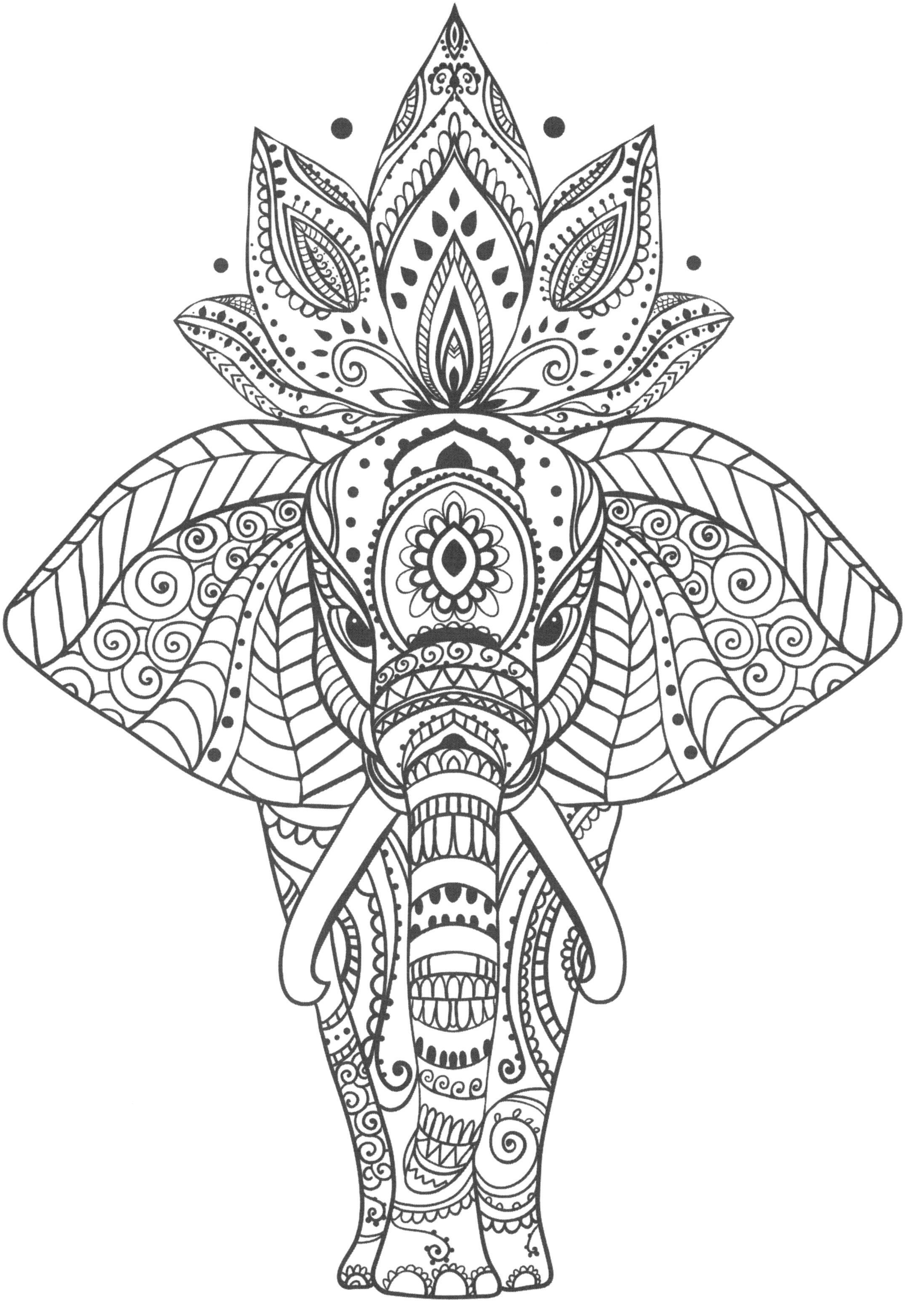

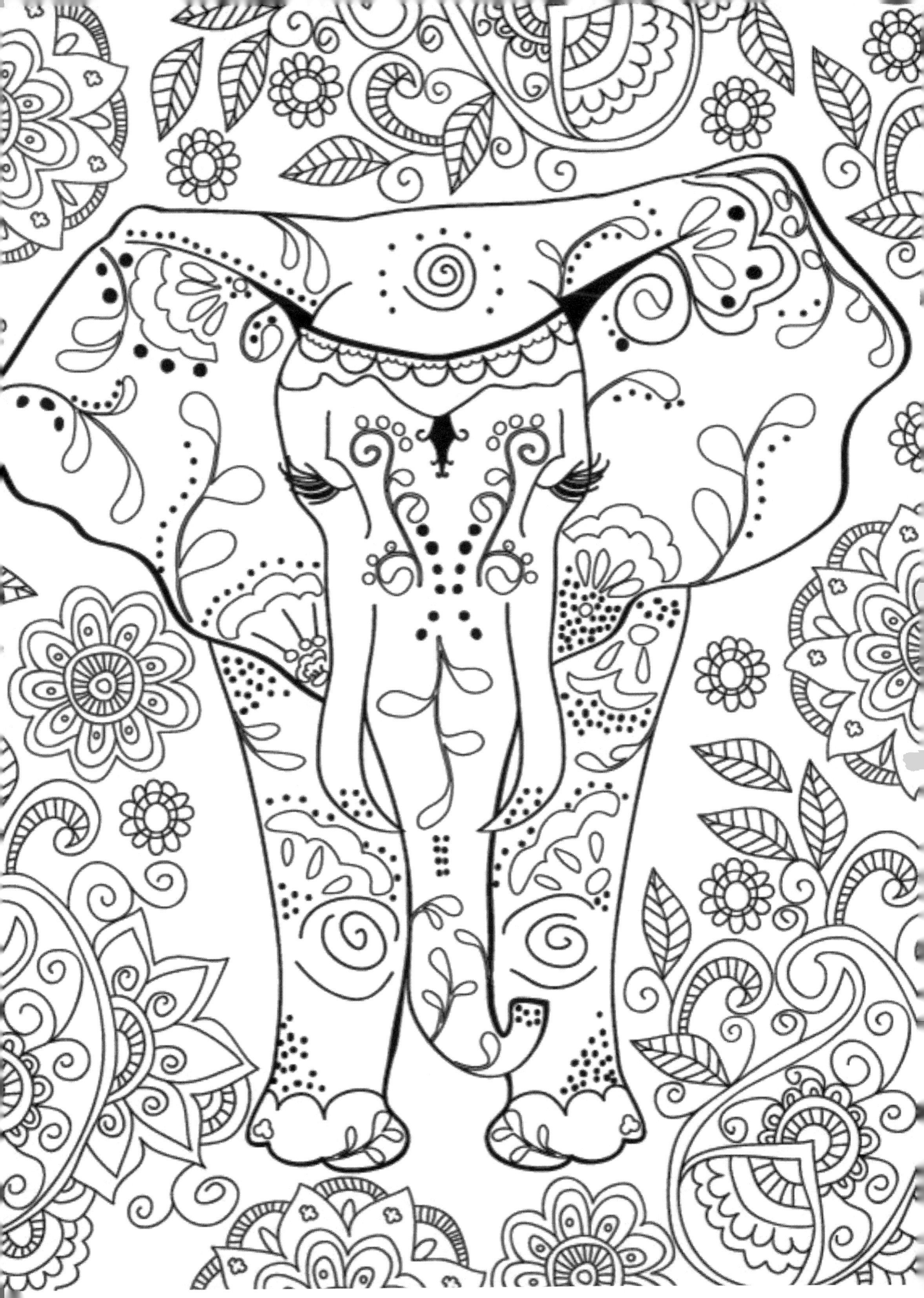

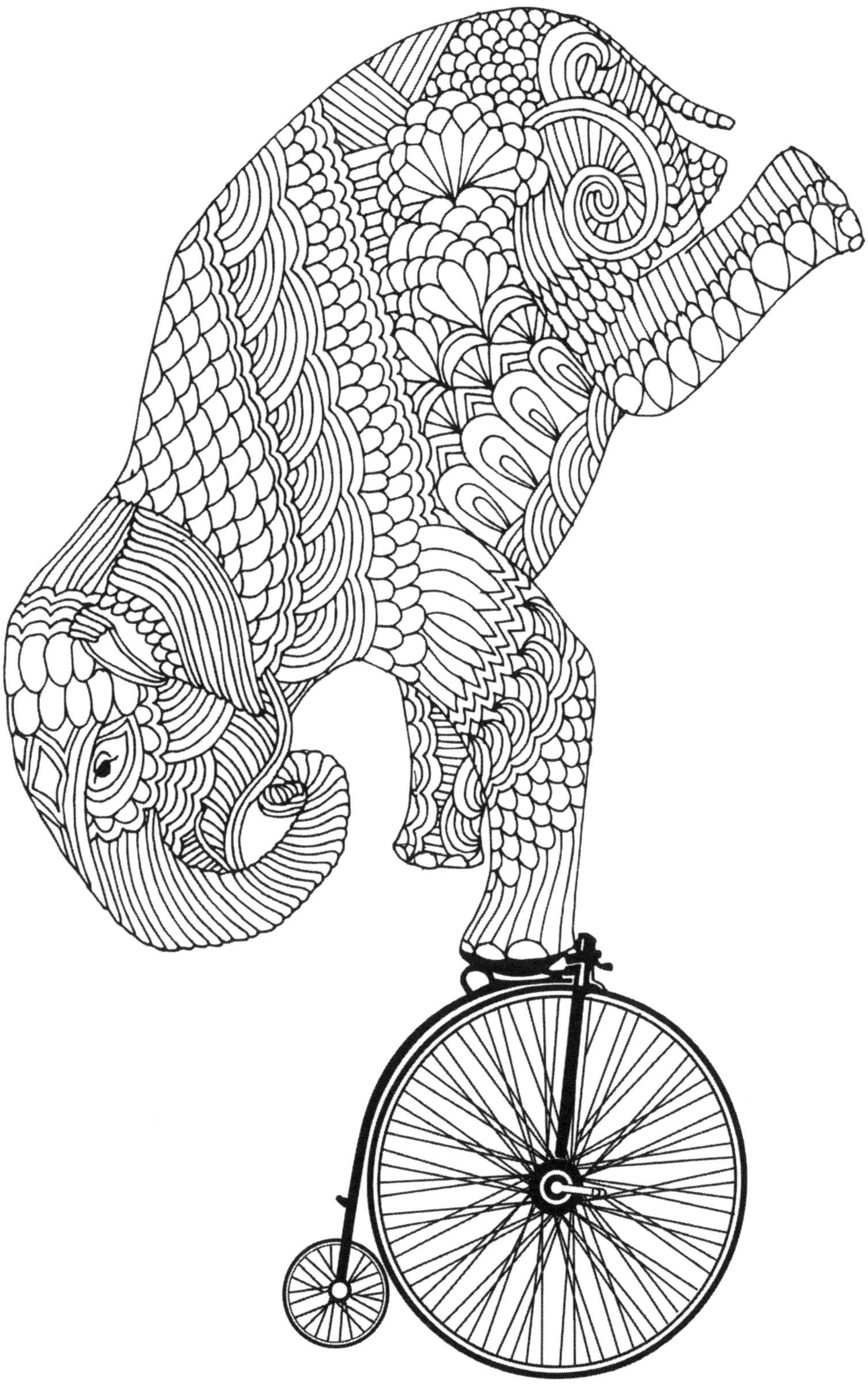

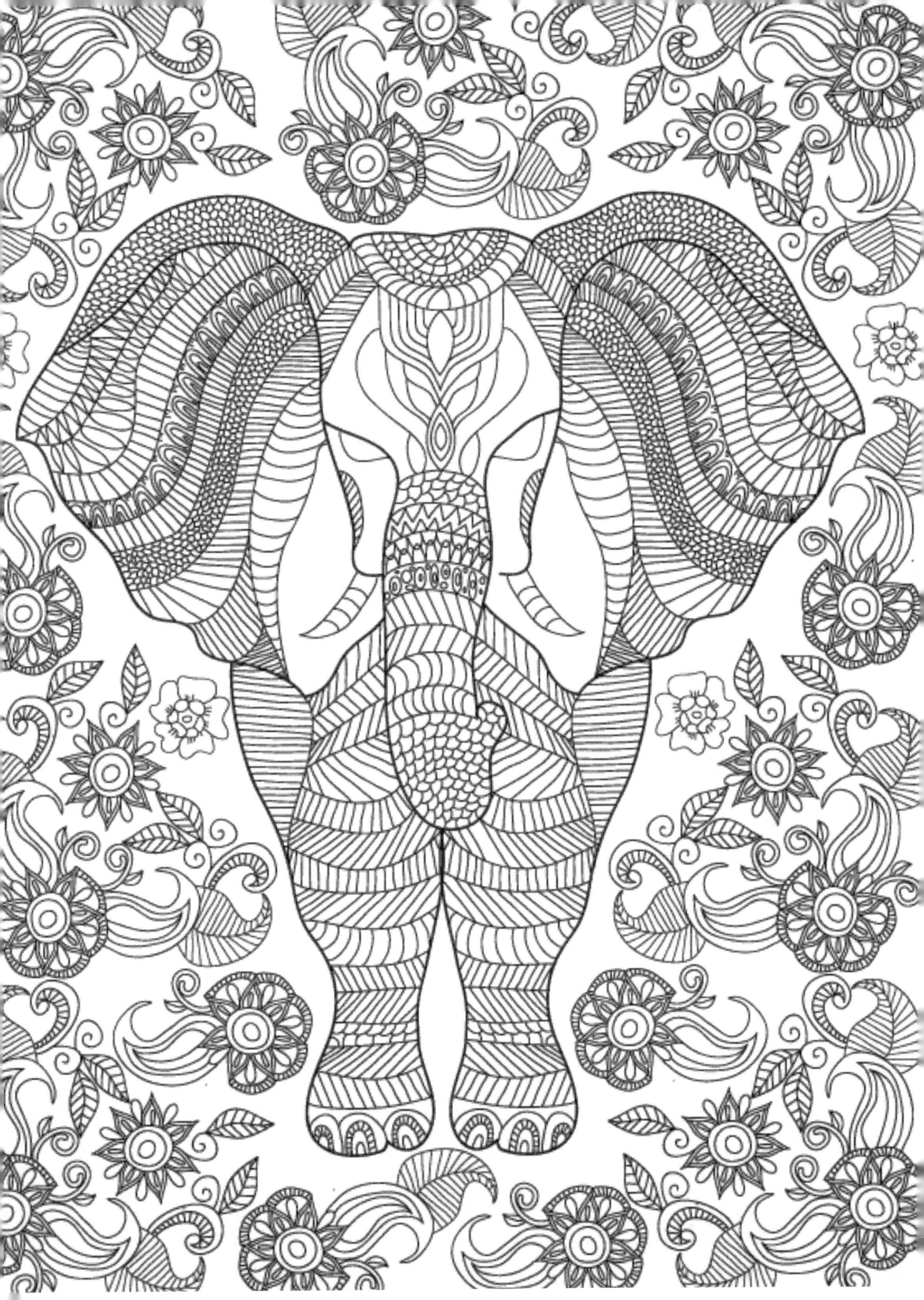

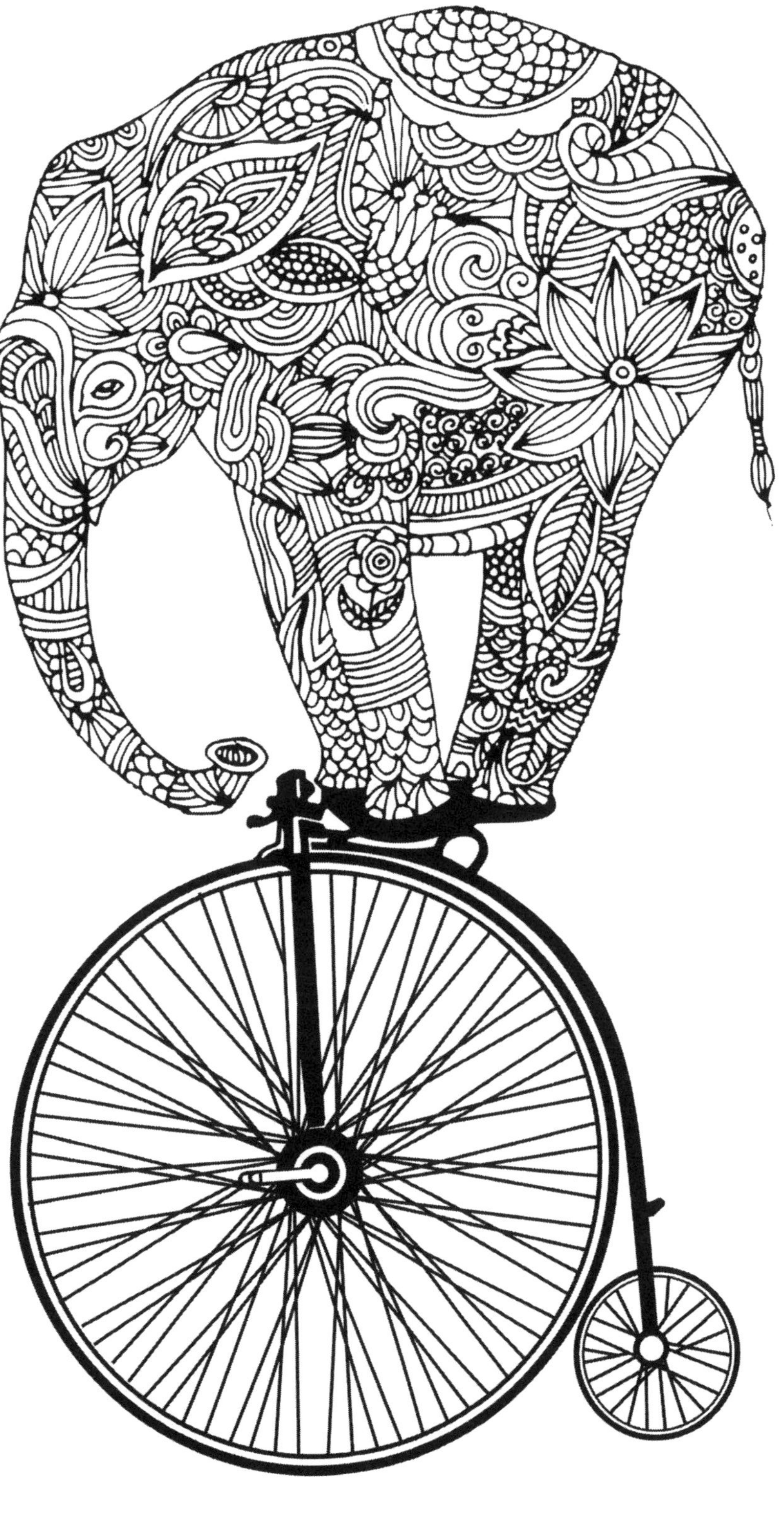

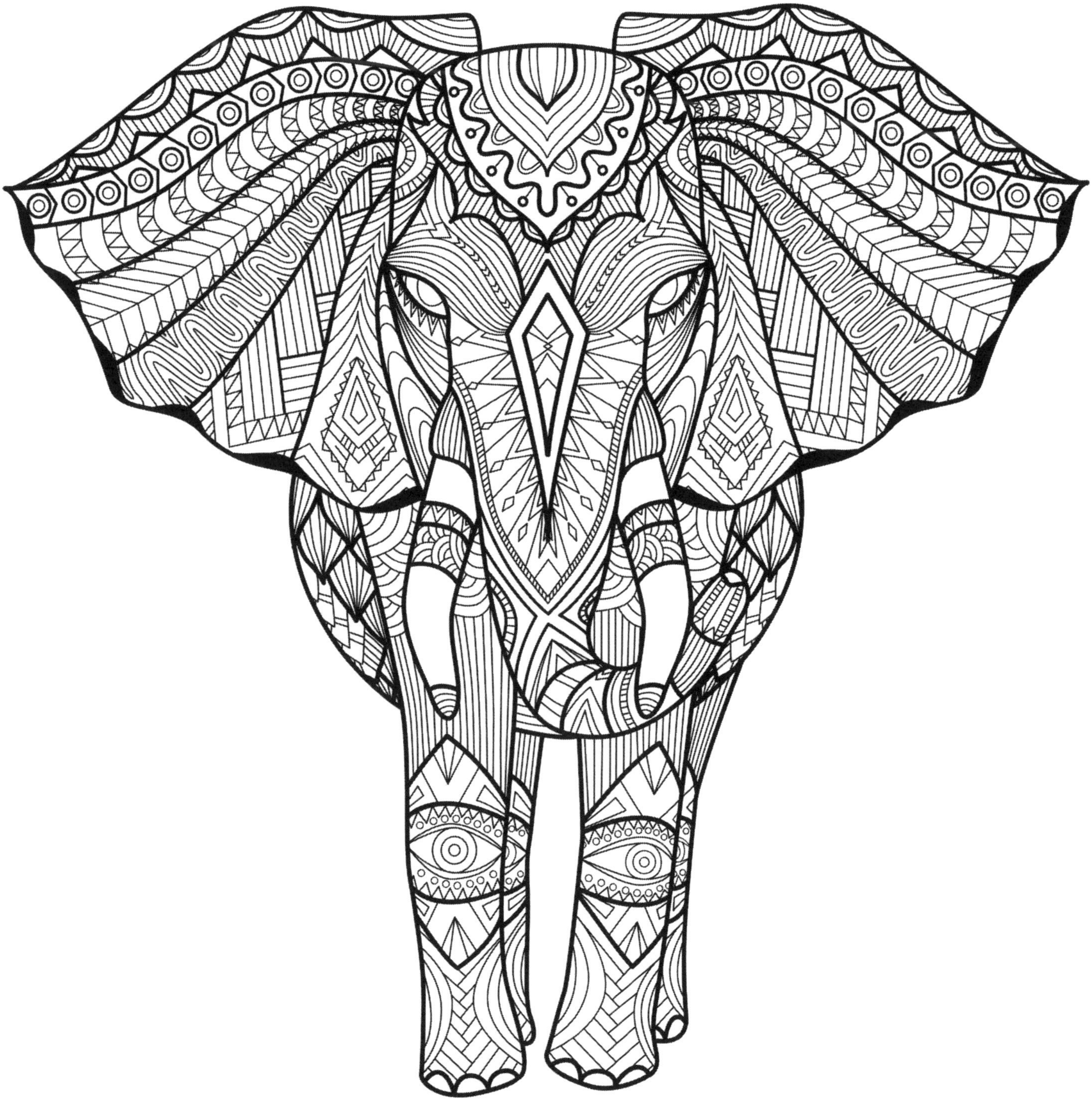

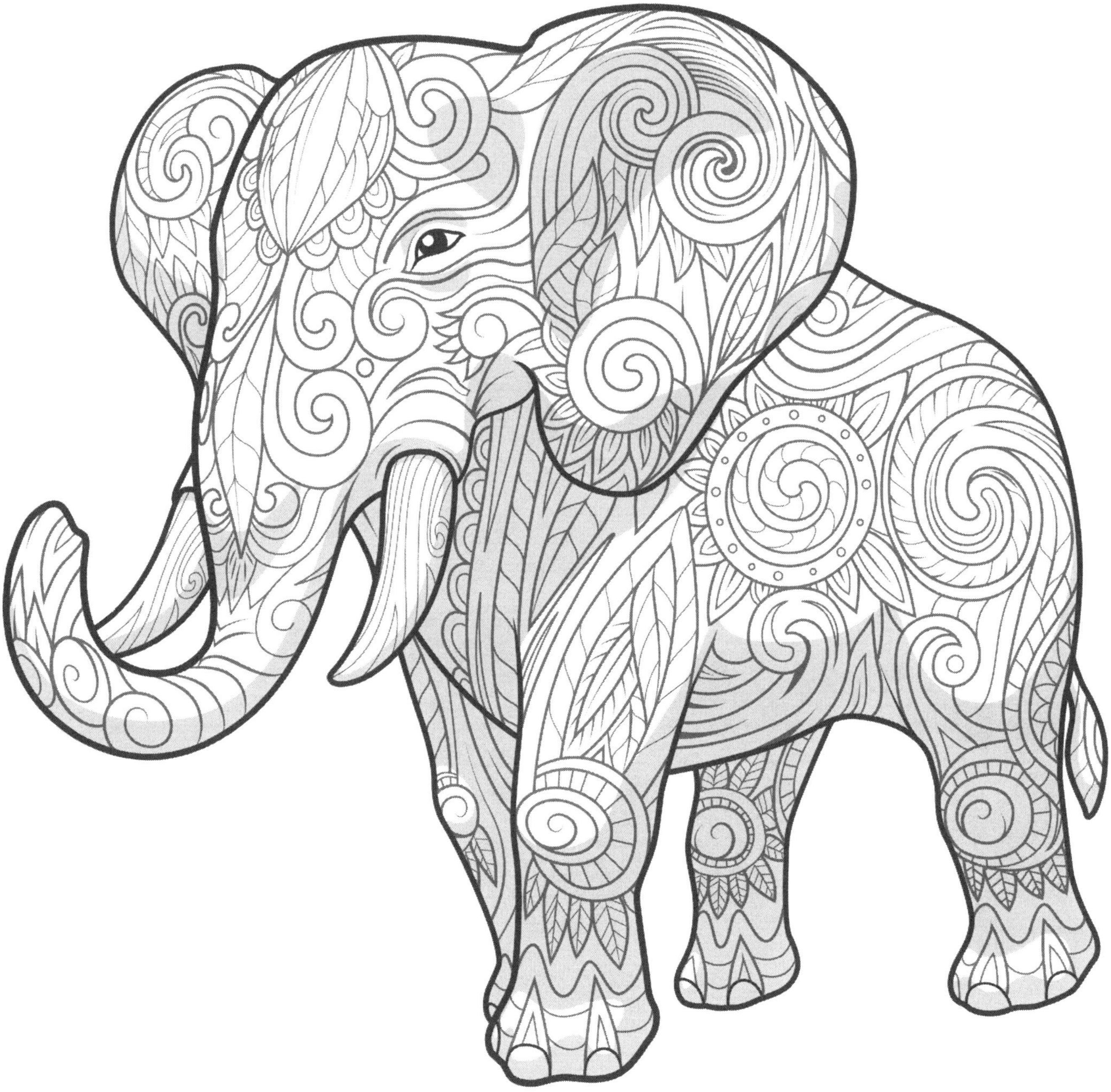

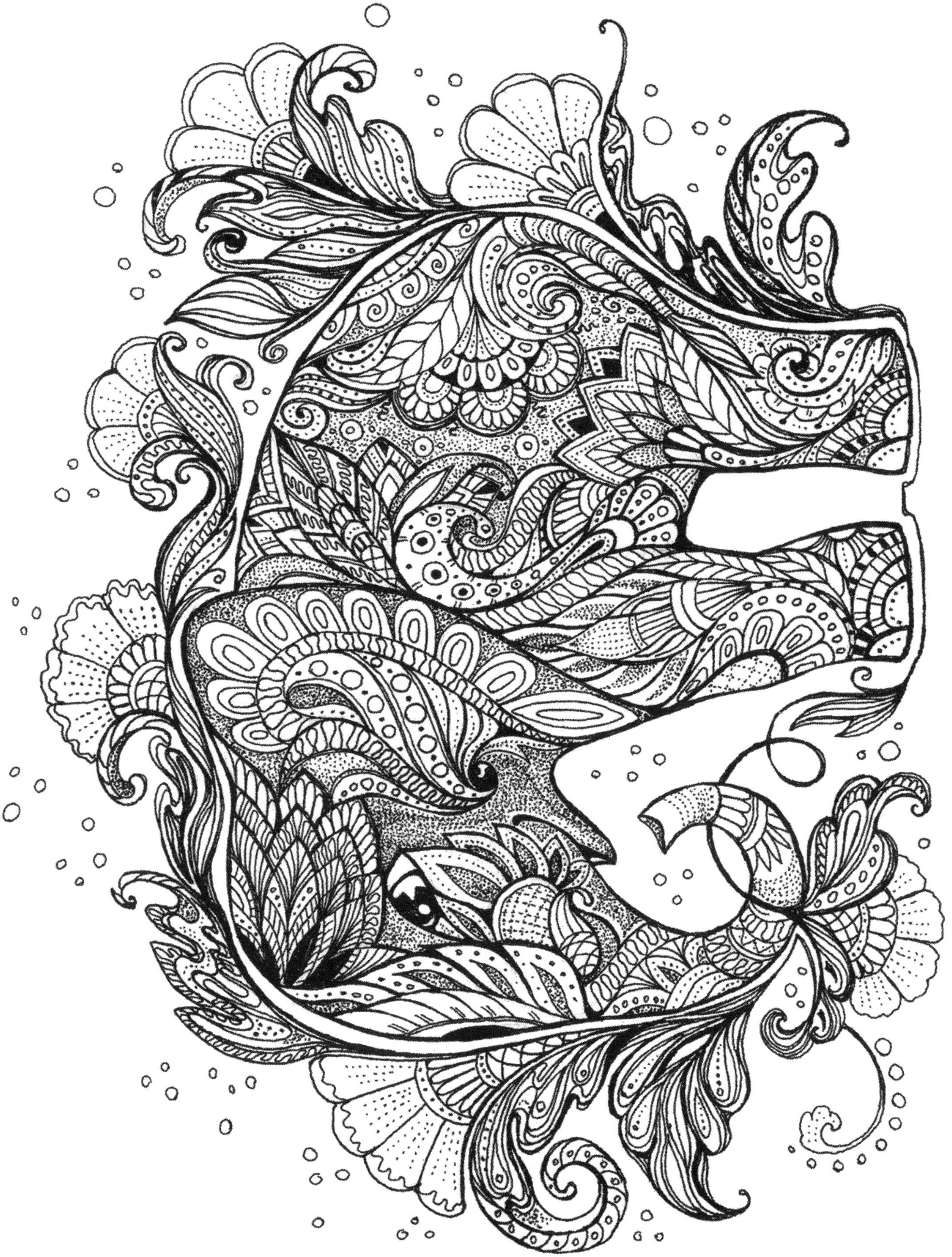

# Thank You

If you enjoyed Coloring this Elegant Elephants, please take a little time to share your thoughts and post a positive review with 5 star rating on Amazon, it would encourage me and make me serve you better. It'd Really be greatly appreciated.

We'll never be perfect, but that won't stop us from trying. Your feedback makes us serve you better. Send ideas, criticism, Compliment or anything else you think we should hear to info@adultscoloringartist.com. We'll Reply you As soon as we receive your Mail. :)

Visit our Author Page to get More Amazing Adults Coloring Books HERE>> https://www.amazon.com/author/adultcoloring

Post Your Completed Colored Pictures on our facebook page here and Subscribe to our News later to get wonderful Bonus Free here>> https://www.facebook.com/pages/Adults-Coloring-Books/839035572846783

Made in the USA
Middletown, DE
12 October 2015